TENOR SAX

101 HIT SONGS

Note: The keys in this book do not match the other wind instruments.

Available for
FLUTE, CLARINET, ALTO SAX, TENOR SAX, TRUMPET,
HORN, TROMBONE, VIOLIN, VIOLA, CELLO

ISBN 978-1-4950-7531-5

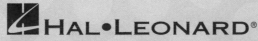

7777 W. BLUEMOUND RD. P.O. BOX 13819 MILWAUKEE, WI 53213

Visit Hal Leonard Online at
www.halleonard.com

CONTENTS

ALL ABOUT THAT BASS

TENOR SAX

Words and Music by KEVIN KADISH
and MEGHAN TRAINOR

AMAZED

TENOR SAX

Words and Music by MARV GREEN,
CHRIS LINDSEY and AIMEE MAYO

ALL OF ME

TENOR SAX

Words and Music by JOHN STEPHENS
and TOBY GAD

Slowly, in 2

APOLOGIZE

TENOR SAX

Words and Music by
RYAN TEDDER

BEAUTIFUL

TENOR SAX

Words and Music by
LINDA PERRY

BAD DAY

TENOR SAX

Words and Music by
DANIEL POWTER

D.S. al Coda

CODA

BAD ROMANCE

TENOR SAX

Words and Music by STEFANI GERMANOTTA
and NADIR KHAYAT

BEAUTIFUL DAY

TENOR SAX

Words by BONO
Music by U2

Moderately

BEAUTIFUL IN MY EYES

TENOR SAX

Words and Music by
JOSHUA KADISON

BECAUSE I LOVE YOU
(The Postman Song)

TENOR SAX

Words and Music by
WARREN BROOKS

BELIEVE

TENOR SAX

Words and Music by BRIAN HIGGINS,
STUART McLENNEN, PAUL BARRY,
STEPHEN TORCH, MATT GRAY
and TIM POWELL

BUTTERFLY KISSES

TENOR SAX

Words and Music by BOB CARLISLE
and RANDY THOMAS

BRAVE

TENOR SAX

Words and Music by SARA BAREILLES
and JACK ANTONOFF

BREAKAWAY

from THE PRINCESS DIARIES 2: ROYAL ENGAGEMENT

TENOR SAX

Words and Music by BRIDGET BENENATE,
AVRIL LAVIGNE and MATTHEW GERRARD

BREATHE

TENOR SAX

Words and Music by HOLLY LAMAR
and STEPHANIE BENTLEY

CALL ME MAYBE

TENOR SAX

Words and Music by CARLY RAE JEPSEN,
JOSHUA RAMSAY and TAVISH CROWE

CANDLE IN THE WIND 1997

TENOR SAX

Words and Music by ELTON JOHN
and BERNIE TAUPIN

Slowly, in 2

CHANGE THE WORLD

featured on the Motion Picture Soundtrack PHENOMENON

TENOR SAX

Words and Music by WAYNE KIRKPATRICK,
GORDON KENNEDY and TOMMY SIMS

CHASING CARS

TENOR SAX

Words and Music by GARY LIGHTBODY,
TOM SIMPSON, PAUL WILSON,
JONATHAN QUINN and NATHAN CONNOLLY

THE CLIMB
from HANNAH MONTANA: THE MOVIE

TENOR SAX

Words and Music by JESSI ALEXANDER
and JON MABE

CLOCKS

TENOR SAX

Words and Music by GUY BERRYMAN,
JON BUCKLAND, WILL CHAMPION
and CHRIS MARTIN

DON'T KNOW WHY

TENOR SAX

Words and Music by
JESSE HARRIS

COUNTDOWN

TENOR SAX

Words and Music by BEYONCÉ KNOWLES,
CAINON LAMB, JULIE FROST, MICHAEL BIVINS,
ESTHER DEAN, TERIUS NASH, SHEA TAYLOR,
NATHAN MORRIS and WANYA MORRIS

2nd time, D.C. al Coda

CODA

CRUISE

TENOR SAX

Words and Music by CHASE RICE,
TYLER HUBBARD, BRIAN KELLEY,
JOEY MOI and JESSE RICE

CRYIN'

TENOR SAX

Words and Music by STEVEN TYLER,
JOE PERRY and TAYLOR RHODES

DIE A HAPPY MAN

TENOR SAX

Words and Music by THOMAS RHETT,
JOE SPARGUR and SEAN DOUGLAS

DILEMMA

TENOR SAX

Words and Music by CORNELL HAYNES,
ANTWON MAKER, KENNETH GAMBLE
and BUNNY SIGLER

Fine

2nd time, D.S. al Fine

DRIFT AWAY

TENOR SAX

Words and Music by
MENTOR WILLIAMS

FIELDS OF GOLD

TENOR SAX

Music and Lyrics by
STING

DROPS OF JUPITER
(Tell Me)

TENOR SAX

Words and Music by PAT MONAHAN,
JAMES STAFFORD, ROBERT HOTCHKISS,
CHARLES COLIN and SCOTT UNDERWOOD

Moderately

FALLIN'

TENOR SAX

Words and Music by
ALICIA KEYS

FIREWORK

TENOR SAX

Words and Music by KATY PERRY,
MIKKEL ERIKSEN, TOR ERIK HERMANSEN,
ESTHER DEAN and SANDY WILHELM

Moderately

FOOLISH GAMES

TENOR SAX

Words and Music by
JEWEL KILCHER

FOREVER AND FOR ALWAYS

TENOR SAX

Words and Music by SHANIA TWAIN
and R.J. LANGE

FRIENDS IN LOW PLACES

TENOR SAX

Words and Music by DeWAYNE BLACKWELL
and EARL BUD LEE

FROM A DISTANCE

TENOR SAX

Words and Music by
JULIE GOLD

GENIE IN A BOTTLE

TENOR SAX

Words and Music by STEVE KIPNER,
DAVID FRANK and PAMELA SHEYNE

GET LUCKY

TENOR SAX

Words and Music by THOMAS BANGALTER,
GUY MANUEL HOMEM CHRISTO, NILE RODGERS
and PHARRELL WILLIAMS

HOW TO SAVE A LIFE

TENOR SAX

Words and Music by JOSEPH KING
and ISAAC SLADE

HELLO

TENOR SAX

Words and Music by ADELE ADKINS
and GREG KURSTIN

HERE AND NOW

TENOR SAX

Words and Music by TERRY STEELE
and DAVID ELLIOT

HERO

TENOR SAX

Words and Music by ENRIQUE IGLESIAS,
PAUL BARRY and MARK TAYLOR

Moderately slow

HEY, SOUL SISTER

TENOR SAX

Words and Music by PAT MONAHAN,
ESPEN LIND and AMUND BJORKLUND

HO HEY

TENOR SAX

Words and Music by JEREMY FRAITES
and WESLEY SCHULTZ

HOLD ON, WE'RE GOING HOME

TENOR SAX

Words and Music by AUBREY GRAHAM,
PAUL JEFFERIES, NOAH SHEBIB,
JORDAN ULLMAN and MAJID AL-MASKATI

HOME

TENOR SAX

Words and Music by GREG HOLDEN
and DREW PEARSON

Moderately, in 2

THE HOUSE THAT BUILT ME

TENOR SAX

Words and Music by TOM DOUGLAS
and ALLEN SHAMBLIN

HOW AM I SUPPOSED TO LIVE WITHOUT YOU

TENOR SAX

Words and Music by MICHAEL BOLTON
and DOUG JAMES

I FINALLY FOUND SOMEONE

from THE MIRROR HAS TWO FACES

TENOR SAX

Words and Music by BARBRA STREISAND,
MARVIN HAMLISCH, R.J. LANGE
and BRYAN ADAMS

I GOTTA FEELING

TENOR SAX

Words and Music by WILL ADAMS,
ALLAN PINEDA, JAIME GOMEZ, STACY FERGUSON,
DAVID GUETTA and FREDERIC RIESTERER

Moderately fast

I KISSED A GIRL

TENOR SAX

Words and Music by KATY PERRY,
CATHY DENNIS, MAX MARTIN
and LUKASZ GOTTWALD

I SWEAR

TENOR SAX

Words and Music by FRANK MYERS
and GARY BAKER

I WILL REMEMBER YOU
Theme from THE BROTHERS McMULLEN

TENOR SAX

Words and Music by SARAH McLACHLAN,
SEAMUS EGAN and DAVE MERENDA

JAR OF HEARTS

TENOR SAX

Words and Music by BARRETT YERETSIAN,
CHRISTINA PERRI and DREW LAWRENCE

JUST THE WAY YOU ARE

TENOR SAX

Words and Music by BRUNO MARS,
ARI LEVINE, PHILIP LAWRENCE,
KHARI CAIN and KHALIL WALTON

Moderately

LIPS OF AN ANGEL

TENOR SAX

Words and Music by AUSTIN WINKLER,
ROSS HANSON, LLOYD GARVEY, MARK KING,
MICHAEL RODDEN and BRIAN HOWES

LITTLE TALKS

TENOR SAX

Words and Music by
OF MONSTERS AND MEN

LET IT GO

TENOR SAX

Words and Music by JAMES BAY
and PAUL BARRY

NEED YOU NOW

TENOR SAX

Words and Music by HILLARY SCOTT,
CHARLES KELLEY, DAVE HAYWOOD
and JOSH KEAR

LOSING MY RELIGION

TENOR SAX

Words and Music by WILLIAM BERRY,
PETER BUCK, MICHAEL MILLS
and MICHAEL STIPE

LOVE SONG

TENOR SAX

Words and Music by
SARA BAREILLES

LOVE STORY

TENOR SAX

Words and Music by
TAYLOR SWIFT

MORE THAN WORDS

TENOR SAX

Words and Music by NUNO BETTENCOURT
and GARY CHERONE

NO ONE

TENOR SAX

Words and Music by ALICIA KEYS,
KERRY BROTHERS, JR. and GEORGE HARRY

100 YEARS

TENOR SAX

Words and Music by
JOHN ONDRASIK

REHAB

TENOR SAX

Words and Music by
AMY WINEHOUSE

THE POWER OF LOVE

TENOR SAX

Words by MARY SUSAN APPLEGATE
and JENNIFER RUSH
Music by CANDY DEROUGE
and GUNTHER MENDE

Slowly

ROAR

TENOR SAX

Words and Music by KATY PERRY,
LUKASZ GOTTWALD, MAX MARTIN,
BONNIE McKEE and HENRY WALTER

Moderately

ROLLING IN THE DEEP

TENOR SAX

Words and Music by ADELE ADKINS
and PAUL EPWORTH

ROYALS

TENOR SAX

Words and Music by ELLA YELICH-O'CONNOR
and JOEL LITTLE

SAVE THE BEST FOR LAST

TENOR SAX

Words and Music by WENDY WALDMAN,
PHIL GALDSTON and JON LIND

SAY SOMETHING

TENOR SAX

Words and Music by IAN AXEL,
CHAD VACCARINO and MIKE CAMPBELL

Very slowly, in 4

SHAKE IT OFF

TENOR SAX

Words and Music by TAYLOR SWIFT,
MAX MARTIN and SHELLBACK

SECRETS

TENOR SAX

Words and Music by
RYAN TEDDER

Moderately slow, in 2

SHE WILL BE LOVED

TENOR SAX

Words and Music by ADAM LEVINE
and JAMES VALENTINE

SMELLS LIKE TEEN SPIRIT

TENOR SAX

Words and Music by KURT COBAIN,
KRIST NOVOSELIC and DAVE GROHL

SOMETHING TO TALK ABOUT
(Let's Give Them Something to Talk About)

TENOR SAX

Words and Music by
SHIRLEY EIKHARD

Moderately

STAY WITH ME

TENOR SAX

Words and Music by SAM SMITH,
JAMES NAPIER, WILLIAM EDWARD PHILLIPS,
TOM PETTY and JEFF LYNNE

STACY'S MOM

TENOR SAX

Words and Music by CHRIS COLLINGWOOD
and ADAM SCHLESINGER

Medium Rock

STAY

TENOR SAX

Words and Music by MIKKY EKKO
and JUSTIN PARKER

STRONGER
(What Doesn't Kill You)

TENOR SAX

Words and Music by GREG KURSTIN,
JORGEN ELOFSSON, DAVID GAMSON
and ALEXANDRA TAMPOSI

2nd time, to Coda

3rd time, Fine

D.S. al Coda

CODA

D.S. al Fine

TEARS IN HEAVEN

TENOR SAX

Words and Music by ERIC CLAPTON
and WILL JENNINGS

TEENAGE DREAM

TENOR SAX

Words and Music by KATY PERRY,
BONNIE McKEE, LUKASZ GOTTWALD,
MAX MARTIN and BENJAMIN LEVIN

Moderately

THINKING OUT LOUD

TENOR SAX

Words and Music by ED SHEERAN
and AMY WADGE

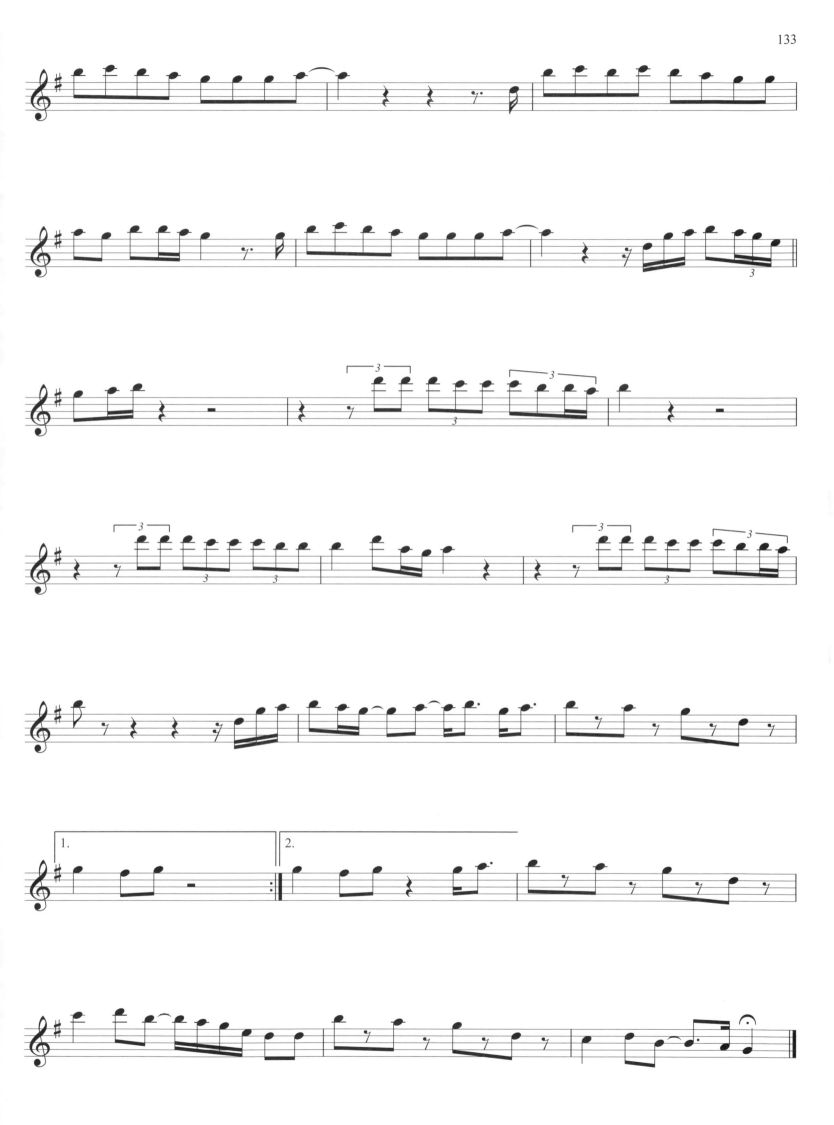

THIS LOVE

TENOR SAX

Words and Music by ADAM LEVINE
and JESSE CARMICHAEL

A THOUSAND YEARS

from the Summit Entertainment film THE TWILIGHT SAGE: BREAKING DAWN - Part 1

TENOR SAX

Words and Music by DAVID HODGES
and CHRISTINA PERRI

TILL THE WORLD ENDS

TENOR SAX

Words and Music by LUKASZ GOTTWALD,
MAX MARTIN, KESHA SEBERT
and ALEXANDER KRONLUND

4th time, to Coda

1.

2.

D.C. al Coda
(take repeat)

CODA

UPTOWN FUNK

TENOR SAX

Words and Music by MARK RONSON,
BRUNO MARS, PHILIP LAWRENCE, JEFF BHASKER, DEVON GALLASPY,
NICHOLAUS WILLIAMS, LONNIE SIMMONS, RONNIE WILSON,
CHARLES WILSON, RUDOLPH TAYLOR and ROBERT WILSON

VIVA LA VIDA

TENOR SAX

Words and Music by GUY BERRYMAN,
JON BUCKLAND, WILL CHAMPION
and CHRIS MARTIN

Moderately

WAITING ON THE WORLD TO CHANGE

TENOR SAX

Words and Music by
JOHN MAYER

WE CAN'T STOP

TENOR SAX

Words and Music by MILEY CYRUS,
THERON THOMAS, TIMOTHY THOMAS, MICHAEL WILLIAMS,
PIERRE SLAUGHTER, DOUGLAS DAVIS and RICKY WALTERS

Moderately slow

WE BELONG TOGETHER

TENOR SAX

Words and Music by MARIAH CAREY,
JERMAINE DUPRI, MANUEL SEAL, JOHNTA AUSTIN,
DARNELL BRISTOL, KENNETH EDMONDS, SIDNEY JOHNSON,
PATRICK MOTEN, BOBBY WOMACK and SANDRA SULLY

WE FOUND LOVE

TENOR SAX

Words and Music by
CALVIN HARRIS

WHAT MAKES YOU BEAUTIFUL

TENOR SAX

Words and Music by SAVAN KOTECHA,
RAMI YACOUB and CARL FALK

WHEN YOU SAY NOTHING AT ALL

TENOR SAX

Words and Music by DON SCHLITZ
and PAUL OVERSTREET

YOU RAISE ME UP

TENOR SAX

Words and Music by BRENDAN GRAHAM
and ROLF LOVLAND

Moderately slow

YEAH!

TENOR SAX

Words and Music by JAMES PHILLIPS,
LA MARQUIS JEFFERSON, CHRISTOPHER BRIDGES,
JONATHAN SMITH and SEAN GARRETT

YOU WERE MEANT FOR ME

TENOR SAX

Words and Music by JEWEL MURRAY
and STEVE POLTZ

YOU'RE BEAUTIFUL

TENOR SAX

Words and Music by JAMES BLUNT,
SACHA SKARBEK and AMANDA GHOST

YOU'RE STILL THE ONE

TENOR SAX

Words and Music by SHANIA TWAIN
and R.J. LANGE

YOU'VE GOT A FRIEND IN ME
from Walt Disney's TOY STORY

TENOR SAX

Music and Lyrics by
RANDY NEWMAN

101 SONGS

BIG COLLECTIONS OF FAVORITE SONGS ARRANGED FOR SOLO INSTRUMENTALISTS.

101 BROADWAY SONGS
00154199	Flute	$14.99
00154200	Clarinet	$14.99
00154201	Alto Sax	$14.99
00154202	Tenor Sax	$14.99
00154203	Trumpet	$14.99
00154204	Horn	$14.99
00154205	Trombone	$14.99
00154206	Violin	$14.99
00154207	Viola	$14.99
00154208	Cello	$14.99

101 HIT SONGS
00194561	Flute	$16.99
00197182	Clarinet	$16.99
00197183	Alto Sax	$16.99
00197184	Tenor Sax	$16.99
00197185	Trumpet	$16.99
00197186	Horn	$16.99
00197187	Trombone	$16.99
00197188	Violin	$16.99
00197189	Viola	$16.99
00197190	Cello	$16.99

101 CHRISTMAS SONGS
00278637	Flute	$14.99
00278638	Clarinet	$14.99
00278639	Alto Sax	$14.99
00278640	Tenor Sax	$14.99
00278641	Trumpet	$14.99
00278642	Horn	$14.99
00278643	Trombone	$14.99
00278644	Violin	$14.99
00278645	Viola	$14.99
00278646	Cello	$14.99

101 JAZZ SONGS
00146363	Flute	$14.99
00146364	Clarinet	$14.99
00146366	Alto Sax	$14.99
00146367	Tenor Sax	$14.99
00146368	Trumpet	$14.99
00146369	Horn	$14.99
00146370	Trombone	$14.99
00146371	Violin	$14.99
00146372	Viola	$14.99
00146373	Cello	$14.99

101 CLASSICAL THEMES
00155315	Flute	$14.99
00155317	Clarinet	$14.99
00155318	Alto Sax	$14.99
00155319	Tenor Sax	$14.99
00155320	Trumpet	$14.99
00155321	Horn	$14.99
00155322	Trombone	$14.99
00155323	Violin	$14.99
00155324	Viola	$14.99
00155325	Cello	$14.99

101 MOVIE HITS
00158087	Flute	$14.99
00158088	Clarinet	$14.99
00158089	Alto Sax	$14.99
00158090	Tenor Sax	$14.99
00158091	Trumpet	$14.99
00158092	Horn	$14.99
00158093	Trombone	$14.99
00158094	Violin	$14.99
00158095	Viola	$14.99
00158096	Cello	$14.99

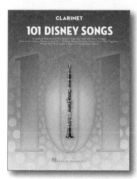

101 DISNEY SONGS
00244104	Flute	$16.99
00244106	Clarinet	$16.99
00244107	Alto Sax	$16.99
00244108	Tenor Sax	$16.99
00244109	Trumpet	$16.99
00244112	Horn	$16.99
00244120	Trombone	$16.99
00244121	Violin	$16.99
00244125	Viola	$16.99
00244126	Cello	$16.99

101 POPULAR SONGS
00224722	Flute	$16.99
00224723	Clarinet	$16.99
00224724	Alto Sax	$16.99
00224725	Tenor Sax	$16.99
00224726	Trumpet	$16.99
00224727	Horn	$16.99
00224728	Trombone	$16.99
00224729	Violin	$16.99
00224730	Viola	$16.99
00224731	Cello	$16.99

HAL•LEONARD®
www.halleonard.com

Prices, contents and availability subject to change without notice.

101 TIPS FROM HAL LEONARD

STUFF ALL THE PROS KNOW AND USE

Ready to take your skills to the next level? These books present valuable how-to insight that musicians of all styles and levels can benefit from. The text, photos, music, diagrams and accompanying audio provide a terrific, easy-to-use resource for a variety of topics.

  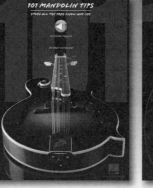  

101 HAMMOND B-3 TIPS
by Brian Charette
Topics include: funky scales and modes; unconventional harmonies; creative chord voicings; cool drawbar settings; ear-grabbing special effects; professional gigging advice; practicing effectively; making good use of the pedals; and much more!
00128918 Book/Online Audio $14.99

101 HARMONICA TIPS
by Steve Cohen
Topics include: techniques, position playing, soloing, accompaniment, the blues, equipment, performance, maintenance, and much more!
00821040 Book/Online Audio $16.99

101 CELLO TIPS—2ND EDITION
by Angela Schmidt
Topics include: bowing techniques, non-classical playing, electric cellos, accessories, gig tips, practicing, recording and much more!
00149094 Book/Online Audio $14.99

101 FLUTE TIPS
by Elaine Schmidt
Topics include: selecting the right flute for you, finding the right teacher, warm-up exercises, practicing effectively, taking good care of your flute, gigging advice, staying and playing healthy, and much more.
00119883 Book/CD Pack.................................$14.99

101 SAXOPHONE TIPS
by Eric Morones
Topics include: techniques; maintenance; equipment; practicing; recording; performance; and much more!
00311082 Book/CD Pack.................................$15.99

101 TRUMPET TIPS
by Scott Barnard
Topics include: techniques, articulation, tone production, soloing, exercises, special effects, equipment, performance, maintenance and much more.
00312082 Book/CD Pack.................................$14.99

101 UPRIGHT BASS TIPS
by Andy McKee
Topics include: right- and left-hand technique, improvising and soloing, practicing, proper care of the instrument, ear training, performance, and much more.
00102009 Book/Online Audio $14.99

101 BASS TIPS
by Gary Willis
Topics include: techniques, improvising and soloing, equipment, practicing, ear training, performance, theory, and much more.
00695542 Book/Online Audio $17.99

101 DRUM TIPS—2ND EDITION
Topics include: grooves, practicing, warming up, tuning, gear, performance, and much more!
00151936 Book/Online Audio $14.99

101 FIVE-STRING BANJO TIPS
by Fred Sokolow
Topics include: techniques, ear training, performance, and much more!
00696647 Book/CD Pack.................................$14.99

101 GUITAR TIPS
by Adam St. James
Topics include: scales, music theory, truss rod adjustments, proper recording studio set-ups, and much more. The book also features snippets of advice from some of the most celebrated guitarists and producers in the music business.
00695737 Book/Online Audio $16.99

101 MANDOLIN TIPS
by Fred Sokolow
Topics include: playing tips, practicing tips, accessories, mandolin history and lore, practical music theory, and much more!
00119493 Book/Online Audio $14.99

101 RECORDING TIPS
by Adam St. James
This book contains recording tips, suggestions, and advice learned firsthand from legendary producers, engineers, and artists. These tricks of the trade will improve anyone's home or pro studio recordings.
00311035 Book/CD Pack.................................$14.95

101 UKULELE TIPS
by Fred Sokolow with Ronny Schiff
Topics include: techniques, improvising and soloing, equipment, practicing, ear training, performance, uke history and lore, and much more!
00696596 Book/Online Audio $15.99

101 VIOLIN TIPS
by Angela Schmidt
Topics include: bowing techniques, non-classical playing, electric violins, accessories, gig tips, practicing, recording, and much more!
00842672 Book/CD Pack.................................$14.99

Prices, contents and availability subject to change without notice.

HAL•LEONARD®
www.halleonard.com